Raising a

 RATED FAMILY

in an

X **RATED WORLD**

™

The first book to include Report Cards for your use
(see the tear-outs at the back of the book)

by Brent and Phelecia Hatch

DAWSON
PUBLISHING

D1405383

For information about seminars please write to:
Dawson Publishing, P. O. Box 820
South Pasadena, CA 91031
(626) 441-0368
or go online at www.thehugdr.com

Copyright © 2001 by Brent and Phelecia Hatch

First printing — April 2001
Second printing — July 2001

ISBN No. 0-945713-07-X
Library of Congress No.: 2001116814

Published by: Dawson Publishing
                P. O. Box 820
                South Pasadena, CA 91031
                (626) 441-0368
                www.thehugdr.com

Printed in the USA

Dedication

This book is dedicated to our children: Shane, Chari, Ashlyne, McKay, Dakota, Saige, and Hunter, and to all those who put family above all else.

Table of Contents

Acknowledgments

We owe a special debt of gratitude to those people who took time out of their busy schedules to review this manuscript and give us expert advice. Thanks to Dana and Debbie Suorsa who spent many hours compiling and editing. Thank you to Victoria Graphics for formatting the manuscript and getting it ready to print, and to my oldest son, Shane, for designing the front cover. Many thanks go to Cary and Cambria Inouye for their input. And thanks to Stan and Sharon Miller for sharing their work with us, Todd White for his illlustrations and Christine Caldwell for her photography.

We would like to thank our children for helping us see our faults and helping us practice what we preach. Last, but not least, a big thanks to our parents for raising us the right way and teaching us the importance of family.

Attempt has been made to acknowledge each contributor by name. However, in many instances, authorship was indeterminate. We express deepest appreciation to each person whose writings appear herein. We are sure they share our desire to have their writings reach and inspire as many people as possible.

Brent and Phelecia Hatch

Foreword

Would you take your family on a vacation to the Amazon River and allow your young children to go off by themselves to explore the mysteries of the jungle? No, of course you wouldn't. That would be irresponsible and negligent, right? Yet we send our children out into a ferocious jungle everyday. What jungle? An X-rated jungle.

The unprecedented proliferation and accessibility of violence, vulgar and pornographic information has truly made our society a morally-dangerous jungle into which parents are frightened to send their children off alone.

Yet, alone they must go, while we as parents hope and pray that they will return to us untainted by the ills of this X-rated world.

Is there anything that we as parents can do to guarantee that our children will make their way through this world happy, healthy, and well-adjusted? There are no guarantees, but I firmly believe that the chances of our children safely navigating through this evil world are much higher when we as parents offer them a supportive base of love, support, and training to counter the challenges they will surely face. This can only happen in our homes. We must make our homes learning centers where our children can acquire the necessary tools to combat the evils of this world. In short, we must create a G-Rated, safe haven in our homes where our children can take refuge from this X-Rated world.

– Cary Inouye

The Hatch Family

Seated: Shane, Hunter, Saige, Brent
Standing: McKay, Chari, Phelecia, Ashlyne, Dakota

About the Authors...

Brent and Phelecia Hatch are the parents of seven children. Brent developed "The Hug Card," with his brother which sold 3.5 million cards and generated $7 million in revenues. Brent and Phelecia have been married for 14 years and enjoy the challenges of parenthood.

Raising seven children ranging in ages from 3 months to 14 years has given them the experience needed to create this book. Brent is also an Eagle Scout and has a background in motivational speaking, so he is prepared for every situation. Brent and Phelecia met in college and they have been together, happily married, ever since.

Although Brent's job is running a successful business, his first priority is helping his wife raise healthy, happy, and successful children.

Brent and Phelecia have been known to say, "Anything worth doing requires a lot of work." Anyone with children knows how much work it is. Brent and Phelecia wrote this book primarily to clarify their own views about parenting, and they hope that, because of this effort, other people will acquire some tools to help in raising their own children. No family is perfect!

From the Authors...

Chinese Poem

Nice night in June
Stars shine big moon
In park on bench
With girl in clench
Me say I love
She coo like dove
Me smart me fast
Never let chance pass
Get hitched me say
She say O.K.
Wedding bells ring, ring
Honeymoon everything
Happy man happy wife

Another night in June
Stars shine big moon
Ain't happy no more
Carry baby walk floor
Wife mad she fuss
Me mad me cuss
Life one big spat
Nagging wife bawling brat
Me realize at last
Me too darn fast!!

Anonymous

This poem seemed an appropriate way to begin a book about raising families.

When my wife and I were in the kitchen one day our 2- and 4-year-olds came to us and said, "Come quick and see what we made." Much to our surprise, the kids had dumped three gallons of cotton candy sugar all over the carpets and sofas. They wanted to show us the designs they made. All we could do was laugh. We took the opportunity to appreciate the innocence and creativity of our children. After we watched our children play in the cotton candy sugar, we used the experience to teach them—lovingly—that there are consequences for choices we make. We had them clean up the cotton candy sugar. What a great learning experience for both child and parent. Parents, it is important to choose your battles wisely.

We are constantly learning with our young family and discovering new things every day. We have chosen to share what we are learning with you because we want you to learn from our mistakes and experiences. We hope the information in this book will help you find happiness and help make your family the best family it can be.

Brent and Phelecia Hatch

Read YOUR story in the Hatchs' next books!

The Hatchs' are putting together their next books, *Raising G-Rated Teens in an X-Rated World*, and *The Power of Positive Hugging*. They would like to hear from you.

✓ What kinds of problems have you encountered in raising your teens?
✓ Have you overcome these problems?
✓ What things have you learned in dealing with these problems?
✓ How do you communicate with your teens?
✓ How do you practice what you've learned?
✓ How has your relationship with your teens improved?

There is no limit on how much you write.

Please send your response to:
    Dawson Publishing
    P. O. Box 820
    South Pasadena, CA 91031
    (626) 441-0368
    www.thehugdr.com

There are no guarantees your story will be used and all material sent will become property of Dawson Publishing.

Teaching in the Home

CHAPTER ONE

Teaching in the Home

The most important lessons we can teach our children are in the home. From the day our children are brought home from the hospital, we hold them, love them and nourish them, and this positive caring must continue throughout their lives. Being a good nurturer means taking an active role in teaching them that failure in the home cannot be compensated for by any other success.

Remember, even though raising children can be challenging, it doesn't last forever! Many people who have already raised their families tell us, "Enjoy the time you have with your children, it goes too quickly! Don't wish this time away!"

I'm often asked, "How can you have seven children and still have a smile on your face?" My reply is, "Relish the beautiful moments, positive and negative, that you have with your precious children! You don't have them for very long!"

I've found that happiness comes when you realize you need to be happy with who you are and not what you have. You will never attain true happiness unless you find it within yourself now. Having seven children, I've realized that it is not the *quantity* of time we spend with our children, it's the *quality* of time that is important.

"Success in the Home"

Our communities are made stronger by success in the home. If we don't have success in the home, meaning we don't feel good about ourselves and are unhappy, those feelings are carried outside the home. The home should be the first place everyone feels secure and happy. People should be nurtured in their homes and they should feel safe within their home environment.

Teaching morals and values at home helps create decent human beings. If we do not teach these virtues, our children will seek morals and values elsewhere, whether good or bad. If they are learning bad morals and values, their integrity will be in jeopardy. Failure in the home produces not only a lack of morals and values, but also deprives our children of receiving the love they need and deserve. Spending quality time with our children is imperative, its necessary to help them feel secure, valued and loved.

"Validation"

Another way we can have success in the home is through practicing validation. Validate your children's feelings and encourage them to talk with you about how they are feeling and why they are upset. Know where your children are at all times and be active in their lives. In a child's life there are two major influences: the influence of a parent, or parents, and the influences of the outside world. It is important that a child values parental influence over that of the outside world. When things go wrong, we cannot solely blame our schools, churches, or neighbors. We must examine our own homelife. It's never too late to change. It is easier to give up than to constantly work on building a wholesome, healthy family, but it is imperative that we do. Both husband and wife must be in agreement—especially where raising children is concerned.

"Communication"

Being a good parent requires communication with our children. There are a lot of things that I need to work on as a father and I'm learning all the time. I'm learning from asking questions.

I look at my kids and ask them, "How can I be a better father? What can I do?" Every one of them raises a hand and tells me about something they would like to see me change. One of the problems I have as a young father is a bad temper. I work on controlling this every day and I am getting better. Raising my voice, yelling, and treating my children unkindly are also things on which I need to work. We, as parents, need to listen to our children because we can learn a great deal from them. Many times we don't listen carefully, or really hear what they are trying to say. We think that because we're older, we know more, so it must be done our way. Not only do we need to listen to our children, we need to wisely implement what they tell us. It's not enough to just listen, we need to validate the things they say.

"Their Opinion Matters"

Children are sharp and observant—often sensitive—and love to tell the truth. They are not afraid to speak up, and they will tell you what you're doing wrong or what you should be doing. We can either take the problem and put it aside, or pay attention to it and try to resolve it. This consideration and concern teaches our children that their opinions matter and that we care. I am trying to do these things with our seven children, but I need all the help I can get. I believe that my family, my children and my wife, all working together, are helping me to become a better father and husband.

"Family Night"

In trying to ensure success in our home, my wife, Phelecia, and I have made a decision to have a family meeting at least once a week. We set aside one special night to teach our children the basic fundamentals of life. The things we discuss with our children during "family night" are values—such as honesty, loving one another, self-esteem, courage, etc., and the dangerous effects of drugs. We establish and work on the "theme for the week" and do follow-up at the next meeting. Family Nights have been a wonderful way for our children to learn these basic values and for us, as parents, to improve and polish our parenting skills.

A common theme of our Family Night is service. The joy our neighbors and friends have when one of our kids rakes their leaves or waters their grass is immeasurable. Practicing service to others is teaching them service and gives them a sense of self-worth, and affects our community in ways that we cannot fully evaluate. My wife and I try to help others because, when our children see us doing service for other people, they learn by example to serve others.

Being a good example is another theme often discussed at family night. It is up to parents to teach children to respect others, including their neighbors and elders. Example is a critical part of teaching, so we need to be good examples to our children. *Do as I say and as I do.* When we are good role models for our children, they, in turn, can learn to be good examples to others.

Teaching by example is very powerful. In my wife's case, when teaching our children, Phelecia does a great job teaching by example. I often want them to do as I say, not as I do. I want my children to do what's right, especially in those areas where I may not be doing what's right. For example, I have a problem with swearing, and it is something on which I have been working. My children do not swear and they tell me it is wrong to swear. This is something I am struggling with, and it's OK because I'm not perfect. It's not productive to get discouraged with yourself if you do something wrong. No one in this world is perfect, and it is important for children to realize that their parents are not perfect. When they get older, they could be disappointed when their parents fall off the pedestal. They can grow and learn from their parents' mistakes, when their parents take an active role in teaching them.

We also role-play at family night. We make up situations regarding issues such as drugs, shoplifting or other serious problems. For example, I will pretend I am a stranger trying to get my kids to buy drugs from me. Or, I will pretend I am a stranger trying to get my kids to get in the car with me, or go somewhere with me. Our oldest son will pretend he is one of our younger kid's friends and he will try to persuade them to shoplift, do drugs, drink alcohol, or smoke. Drugs have been a problem in this world for generations, so I started teaching my children about drugs and their ill effects from the time they could speak. I teach them about the terrible effects drugs could have on them and their lives. When we role-play I have the older kids offer the younger kids drugs and try to persuade them to take them.

I specifically create realistic situations with my children and have them act these situations out because I know eventually they will actually be put into these types of situations. An example of this happened recently. My oldest son asked my wife if he could play ball at the park with a friend. My wife agreed, but asked him to be home in an hour. Two hours passed and my son hadn't returned. My wife went to the park looking for him and he wasn't there, so she went to his friend's home. His mother said her husband had taken them to the gas station across the street from the park to get something to drink, and they should be home very soon. My wife thanked her and asked that she send our son home as soon as they got back. Another hour passed and our son still hadn't come home. When he finally did get home he was very frazzled. He told my wife his friend's father did take them to the gas station where he purchased some beer, and then drove them to his workplace in Los Angeles. His friend's father proceeded to drink with his work buddies. My son, Shane, told us he wanted to get away from them as soon as he could, because he knew this man would be driving them home after drinking alcohol. My son said he knew this was wrong because of all of the things we had taught him. He knew he was in a bad situation and didn't like it and wanted to do everything he could to escape it and be back in the safety of his own home.

By role-playing and teaching our children how to respond to these events, whenever they happen, they will do the right thing. It is important to role-play as a family with your children, because at some time in their lives they will be put in a negative situation with drugs or something else that is harmful. I was put in harmful situations as a child, but because I had also done role-playing I knew how to handle myself.

"Role Models"

Good parents are the best role models. Children learn everything by watching their parents. If children don't have positive role models in their families, they should turn to uncles, cousins, or other family members they might feel are positive role models. There are so many dangers in the world, and many dangerous people who will do anything to destroy the family unit. Many of the role models out in the world are generally the wrong role models. People's actions speak louder than their words. One very bad example is former President Bill Clinton. The president is supposed to be someone we would like our children to follow, especially where character is concerned, but he fell far short of that role. Talk about a rotten example. He did something wrong, lied about it and ultimately got away with it. This is teaching our children that it is alright to lie because the consequences won't be that great. The world's standards are not very high and this teaches our children that following lower standards is acceptable.

Many people want to destroy the very nature and foundation of the family because they themselves are unhappy. Once the family structure breaks down, the basic moral values of our nation, as intended by its founders, will also break down. If a house is built upon the sand, the house will eventually fall. If the house is built upon solid rock, it will stand firm. If a family unit is solid, reinforced with good morals, values, honesty and integrity, that family will stand firm. The family unit is the basic foundation of society. When it fails true family happiness cannot be achieved. Our children need to be the very focus of our lives. If they do not have our full attention, they will find it somewhere else...and that would not be a good thing.

"Unconditional Love"

As a parent and/or role model, we must continuously show unconditional love. This is important, and if we do so, our children will trust us and follow our example. Sometimes, for me it's difficult. While I want to show them unconditional love, I also want them to know they must do what's right. Since children are not all the same, different methods of teaching work for different children. Some children can be told what to do, while others need to learn for themselves. Some children need to find out the hard way, like touching a hot pan or fire on the stove. We can tell our children, "Don't touch the stove, you'll get burned." Some children will listen, some will not. Those who don't listen will get burned, but learn their lesson. Others can simply be told, or learn from the mistakes of others. As parents, it's important to remember that our children are always watching us.

"Honesty"

When people called on the phone I would sometimes tell my kids to say I wasn't home. Then I realized this was teaching them to lie. To correct this problem I told them to say, "Yes my parents are home, but they are busy. Can I take a message?" One of the keys to strengthening the family is honesty.

One of the ways we encourage honesty in our children is to have peace and harmony in our home. That is hard to do when so many things from the outside world bombard us. There are many things we can do as a family to strengthen the family unit and make our home a safe place where each of our children feel loved. We need to remember that a soft voice turns away anger, but a loud voice turns away peace. When I'm angry with my kids and raise my voice, everything goes crazy. I'm like a lion—my voice keeps getting louder. When I speak softly—which my wife is always encouraging me to do— our home feels like a home filled with harmony. We encourage our children to love God, read the scriptures, and pray always.

"Spirituality"

Spirituality is lacking in the world today. Children need to know that there is something bigger and more important than clothes, friends, or television. We also fill our home with good, uplifting music. Some of the songs on the radio today are filled with so much hate; we need to know what our children are listening to. Be involved with your children and know what they're doing. In our family we try to listen to church music and things that send good messages to our children. I play the drums and still like to listen to rock 'n roll but, I make sure the music we bring into our home does not reflect the violence and sadness that is out in the world.

"Affection"

One of the best things we can do for our children as a mom and dad is to kiss and hug in front of them. It is important to show affection in front of your children, so they'll know their mom and dad really love and care about each other. This makes children feel safe. There is nothing worse for a child then to feel that their parents don't love each other. There is so much divorce in this country, much more now than ever before. We must not give up on each other. Too many people give up, and that is one of the reasons there is so much divorce. Divorce is hurtful to children, because when the family unit is broken, the world they know is ripped apart. They no longer feel safe. Kids often feel divorce is their fault and this leads to low self-esteem. If your children know that you, as parents, truly love each other, this makes them feel better. Your children will feel safe knowing mom and dad love each other as much as they love the family. It made me feel better when I saw my parents hug. Show them that you love one another. This teaches your children how to respect the opposite sex. They will learn how to treat their future spouse by the way you and your spouse treat each other. Remember, children learn by example.

True happiness does not come from how big your house is or the size of your paycheck. It is how you feel in your heart. The greatest assets we have are our children, they are our legacy. Whenever possible have a sit-down dinner. It is a time of growing, a time for sitting and listening to your kids. A lot of teaching can be done at the table. On Sunday we will pick one child and everyone has to say something positive about that person. The kids need to express themselves as much as possible.

"Speak Kind Words"

I tell my children not to be mean to others. An acquaintance of mine told me about a fight he had with his brother. This man told his brother that he hated him and couldn't stand him. It's not important why they were mad at each other because, chances are, it was a petty reason. Later that day, while on a bike, his brother was hit by a car and killed. My acquaintance has never forgiven himself and now, as an adult, wishes he'd never said those things. He is haunted by this, but can never take his offensive words back. Kids often say things that they don't mean, but might later regret. I am constantly working with my children to make sure positive things are said in our home. For every negative thing we say in our home, we must say ten positive things to make it even. If our kids fight, we always make sure they hug and make up, no matter what, because it is important. It is important for children to learn to apologize because it helps them not be resentful and angry. It is hard to stay mad at someone when you are being kind to them. Our children need to know it is OK to be upset, but they also need to learn that anger has a time and place. This also teaches them how to compromise. If you teach your children to hug and make up, they will understand how to reach an agreement that also helps to minimize resentment and anger.

The following story is one I once read, that has affected how I deal with our children.

The Meanest Mother[1]

Reprinted with permission
Published by Bookcraft, 1971-1999

"I had the meanest mother in the whole world. While other kids ate candy for breakfast, I had to have cereal, eggs or toast. When others had cokes and candy for lunch, I had to eat a sandwich. As you can guess, my supper was different from the other kids' also.

But, at least I wasn't alone in my sufferings, my sister and two brothers had the same mean mother that I had.

My mother insisted on knowing where we were at all times. You'd think we were on a chain gang. She had to know who our friends were and what we were doing. She insisted that if we said we'd be gone for one hour that we would be gone one hour or less, not one hour and one minute. I am nearly ashamed to admit it, but she actually struck us. She didn't strike us just once, but each time we did as we pleased. Can you imagine someone actually hitting a child just because he disobeyed? Now you can begin to see how mean she was.

The worst is yet to come. We had to be in bed by nine o'clock each night, and up early the next morning. We couldn't sleep till noon like our friends. So while they slept, my mother actually had the nerve to break the child labor law—she made us work. We had to wash dishes, make beds, learn to cook and all sorts of cruel things. I believe she laid awake at night thinking up mean things to do to us.

She always insisted upon our telling the truth, the whole truth and nothing but the truth, even if it killed us—and it nearly did.

By the time we were teenagers, she was much wiser, and our life became even more unbearable. None of this tooting the horn of a car for us to come running. She embarrassed us to no end by making our dates and friends come to the door to get us. I forgot to mention, while my friends were dating at the mature age of 12 and 13, my old-fashioned mother refused to let me date until the age of 15 or 16. At age 15, that is, if I dated only to go to a school function, and that was only once or twice a year.

My mother was a complete failure as a mother. None of us has ever been arrested, divorced or beaten his mate. Each of my brothers served his time in the service of his country. And who do we have to blame for the terrible way we turned out? You're right, our mean mother. Look at all the things we missed! We never got to march in a protest parade, nor to take part in a riot, burn draft cards, or a million and one other things that our friends did. She forced us to grow up into God-fearing, educated, honest adults.

Using her as an example, I am trying to properly raise my three children. I stand a little taller and I am filled with pride when my children call me mean, because, you see, I thank God that he gave me the meanest mother in the whole world."

Tearing

D
o
w
n

Walls

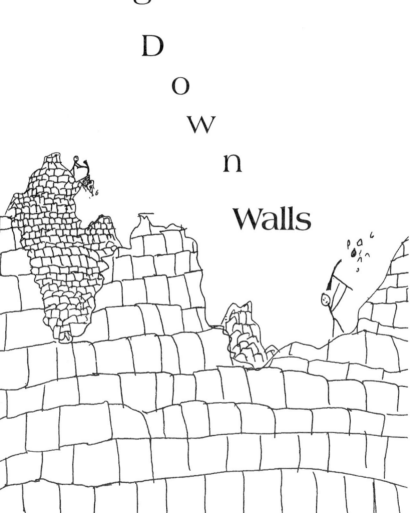

CHAPTER TWO

Tearing Down Walls

Walls[1]

The bricks go up one by one
With words unsaid and deeds undone
The longer we lie dumb
The stronger the walls become

No words exchanged
Relationships estranged
Living side by side
So many feelings to hide

Do the trouble to seek
Find that brick weak

Years of hurt to undo
Time to break through

Cambria Inouye

The power of love has tremendous power to tear down invisible walls! You may notice as our children get older they are not as easy to talk with. It may feel like there is an invisible wall there, which, at times, makes it harder to communicate with them. As parents, we wonder why don't they talk to us like they used to?

Parents, you are not alone in your feelings. As parents, we know all too well how children can build walls around themselves. Children choose to build walls for a lot of reasons. Sometimes, they build them from feelings of being misunderstood, or not trusting, or to protect themselves.

What is the first step on how to break down such walls? How do we talk to our children who really may not want to talk to us? What are some ways to make ourselves the type of parents our children will want to share their feelings with?

There was a time when our family was just finishing a three-day vacation, and were getting into the car to go home. My teenage son told me he was very angry with his father, and he was saying very mean and hurtful remarks about him. Our son is usually a very kind person, so I was very shocked and hurt. Instead of getting defensive, I knew I needed to hear the feelings behind the words he was saying. So, calmly, I asked him to talk to me alone. We were able to share our feelings, and he was able to open up and tell me why he was feeling the way he was. That was such a beautiful experience in communicating effectively. I had been able to look over the wall and hear the crying on the other side.

Do you love me? Do you care about me? Am I important in your life? Questions like these never come directly from your children, but they do come. The most vital part of good communication is to hear what isn't being said. Children's needs and emotions are most often expressed in coded messages that we must receive and interpret.

Remember when your child was a newborn and when he cried you would wonder why. Your thoughts were "if he could only tell me what he needs." As our children grow older, it is still difficult for them to express their needs clearly. They give off signs that you, as parents, must figure out what they need. It is like, in their own way, they are still crying, only now the tears are on the inside. Children will drop hints to see how you will react. If we act too harshly or judgmental, our children will not want to open up to us. As parents, we must look over the wall and hear the cry.

Find the Loose Brick

Brick walls all have loose bricks. We all have weaknesses. In your child's armor, there will be a flaw. Find that weakness and then slowly tap away at it until you can gain entrance into your child's life. When a child has built a wall to surround himself, find the one interest or ability that will allow you to get through that wall. Some of these interests may include basketball, soccer, sports, art, bike riding or computers. When you locate that one lose brick, it is just a matter of taking the time to push and pull at it until the wall is penetrated.

Communicating effectively is the answer to complete destruction of the walls that children build around themselves. The three important elements of opening up communication are respect, love and trust.

Some of the reasons parents have a hard time talking with their children is the way love is communicated. We seem to take on more of a "boss" role when exercising authority, or demanding accountability and then, if they comply and earn a good enough "track record," we show our love and approval. We must constantly show love and caring, always given freely and first, through failure or success. Even if we don't approve of the choices our children make, they always need unconditional love

The way to nourish relationships is by allowing freedom and by keeping confidences. Complementing young people is another way to attain trust. Sometimes, as parents, we tend to block the doors of communication that we so want our children to enter through. It is essential not to put down our children. These words can hurt deep down for a very long time Young people also need respect. It also allows for open communication—respect begets respect. Communication with our children will improve in direct proportion to the amount of respect we show them.

The tearing down of these invisible walls takes a lot of

effort and individual attention. We need to look over these walls and find the loose bricks or tear down the walls completely. We must find the best ways to touch the person behind the wall.

Discipline

CHAPTER THREE

Discipline

Building Love[1]

It's building with love day by day
It's helping by showing the way
It's being parents working together
It's setting limits to make them better
It's helping the child grow
Because sometimes the answer has to be no

Cambria Inouye

Discipline is very important. I remember that as I was writing this book my 2-year-old tried to pull the papers I was working with off the table. I asked her not to touch Daddy's papers, but she continued to grab for them. After the third time, I knew I couldn't reason with a two-year-old, so I decided to discipline her. Everyone disciplines differently, but one way I discipline my children is to give them a little swat on the rear end. She was going to do it again, but she thought twice about doing it and decided not to. It is so important to discipline our children with love. So many people don't believe in discipline and that is one of the reasons we have so many troubled children today. They need to be disciplined continually. Discipline is teaching your child out of love, not punishing him out of anger.

Sometimes my children don't understand why they receive discipline. I let them know the choices they make are their choices, and that they have to pay the consequences if their choices are bad ones. Discipline is a way to show your children you care about them because you want them to succeed in this world. Discipline is for the sake of the child as well as the parent. Discipline teaches children how to follow rules. Children do not like to feel out of control, but without discipline, children can tend to feel out of control. Children need responsible adults to teach them right from wrong. Every time our children make bad choices, I send them to their room and let them think about what they've done for a while. Then I go in and give them a hug. I tell them I love them and that as a parent if I didn't care about them I would let them do whatever they wanted.

In April 1999, the world watched in horror the terrible Columbine High School massacre. I asked myself the question, "What could I do as a parent to discipline my children in a way that would let them know that I love them enough to show them what's right?"

Part of discipline is supervision. Supervision is very important. Teaching our children to do what's right involves knowing where they are, and what they are doing, whenever possible. If you have constant communication with your child, you will be able to help him avoid damaging situations. Here is an example:

A letter from a Child Molester

Phelecia and I came across a letter that was written by a child molester to warn parents against people like himself.

In the letter he stated he was an average-looking individual who could be the guy next door. He is the person you trust, such as a family member, neighbor, even a pastor.

The best warning he could give to parents, he said, is this: "If any adult is spending large amounts of time with your child there is a reason and it may be a bad one. Be aware of anyone wanting to take your child to the movies, an amusement park, or overnight trips alone. You don't know what their motives are."

He said it is important to ask your child questions if this is happening to them. Your children may lie because they are afraid of what the molester may do to them. They may also be afraid that their parents will be upset with them.

He told of his own molestation and the lies he told his parents for fear of punishment. The molesting continued for years and his life was destroyed. He knows now that had he told his parents, he could have stopped this cycle before it went further and his life would not have been ruined. Also, he would not have become a molester, himself, and ruined the lives of others.

He wanted everyone to know that he sought after single mothers who enjoyed the freedom he provided. The children enjoyed the attention and enjoyed having a friend. ***He warned... if your child is lonely, he is a molester's dream.***

His best piece of advice was for grandparents, parents, aunts and uncles to talk to their children and educate them about the dangers of child molesters. There is a 1 in 4 chance that a child who was molested will become a molester.

He strongly suggests you ask questions that your child will answer truthfully and not avoid. Never blame your child and always show your child you love them.

And always remember: If an adult is spending large amounts of time with your child, find out why. There may be a problem.

Anonymous

"Learning a Lesson"

I know that my parents played a big part in my life and knew 99% of the time what I was doing. After a date I had to let them know what I did, what happened, and where I went.

I remember as a young boy of 8-9 years of age I came home from school, and my friend told me to lie about a model car that I paid for. I wanted my parents to think I won it at school so they would be proud of me. Unbeknown to me, my parents heard us talk about the lie. Later that day I remember going to the park. All of us were getting out to play soccer (that was my favorite game), but before I got out of the car, my Dad said, "I know you didn't win the model car, you bought it. You can't play with the other kids. You need to think about what you did." I was so mad at my parents for not letting me play at first, but I was more upset with myself for not being honest.

Not too long ago my oldest son, Shane, and oldest daughter, Chari, were over at a good friend's house and they were being rude to our friends. Apparently, Shane and Chari were disciplined for something they had done and didn't like the discipline they received. In response, Shane and Chari were rude to our friends. When we were told, my wife and I were very upset about the way our children had acted. We listened to our children's side of the story, but told them no matter what they did or didn't do, it was not OK to disrespect adults. We made them apologize and do some chores around the house. We told both of our kids we love them, but as parents we were not going to be easy on them.

Another side to discipline is remembering to award the good behavior. When our children are good they are rewarded for it, either through verbal affirmation or affection. This helps them seek the good attention and not the bad.

"T.V. Time"

Sometimes we can do things to prevent the act of discipline. One of the best things we did in our home was put a time limit on the TV watching and video games. We found our children were more disagreeable with one another, and with us, when a lot of television was watched or a lot of time was spent playing video games. At first it is very hard to break a habit of lots of TV watching, but remember, you are the parent. Many parents give in to their kids. It's hard at first, but if you are persistent you can have a huge influence on your children. There are so many wonderful programs on television today that are uplifting and educational, but for every good show there seems to be five that are unacceptable for children, or adults, to watch. These unacceptable programs, when allowed in the home, not only bring in a negative attitude, but teach our children bad principles. Even though good programming can be very educational, we need to make sure that we, as parents, are the ones who teach our children good morals and values.

I believe that our kids need to be kids, but they also need to know reality. It is difficult for our children to learn about life and work when they spend all of their free time watching television or playing video games. I was taught to work hard and learned that hard work is very good for the soul. I grew up on a farm so I had chores I needed to do. My parents needed our help to get the work done, so we were expected to pitch in. This taught me responsibility, endurance, and brought good self-esteem, which are all important attributes to teach our children. Here are some statistics that are very scary about TV.

- More than 30 million children watch TV unsupervised every day.

- Crime makes up ¼ of all local news coverage.

- 47% of American children have a TV in their bedroom.

- 2/3 of all Prime-time television programs contain violence.

- A child will see 100,000 violent acts on TV by the end of Elementary School.

- The average child from ages 2 to 11 watches television for 1,197 minutes each week.

(TV Free America)[3]

I believe shows that are uplifting and that have a positive effect on kids are great and are also badly needed. If we are constantly supervising our children we will know what type of shows they are watching. From a young age, the effects of television and other things which we see last a lifetime. It was hard for my wife and I at first, because we had to take the first step and slowly take the TV away from the kids. Nowadays, we spend a lot more time together as a family, and the kids read more. Also, the disagreements are fewer and there is more peace in our home.

Whenever my wife and I go out, we leave videos that we know are good and uplifting for our children to watch. They should not be watching shows with violence, nudity, or bad language. They need to see things with kindness and happiness. If you work outside the home, it's important to know what is going on in your home as far as the TV is concerned. Remember, we are the parents. As a parent I used to negotiate with my kids. I got nowhere. Now, I set the rules and limits on my children.

Unconditional
LOVE

CHAPTER FOUR

Unconditional Love

Quality Time[1]

I take her little face into my hands
Deeply I look into her eyes
She returns the gaze
Her beautiful brown eyes
Looking back into mine
I say strongly but softly,
"I love you forever
unconditionally my
beautiful girl."
And stare a bit longer
So that what I said
Before is unspoken but
Felt deep in her soul.

Cambria Inouye

Unconditional love is so important for children. Children need to understand that no matter what they do, or how they act, their parents will love them. One way we show our children unconditional love is through respect. We treat them as individuals with individual ideas. We listen to them and validate their feelings. Everyone needs to be validated, especially children. If they are feeling sad, tell them you are sorry they feel sad. Don't dismiss their feelings.

"Build Each Other Up"

Another way we show unconditional love is by not yelling at our children. No one likes to be yelled at. If you treat your children kindly, they will treat you kindly in return, and they will want to be obedient and do what you ask them to do. We must also avoid words that demean, tear down, disappoint or discourage. We teach our children to avoid damaging habits when we choose to use words that build, praise, compliment and uplift. We must always speak kind words to each other.

Inviting your children to express their thoughts and being positive about those thoughts helps create a learning environment. A good rule to apply to this principle is, "ask, don't tell." Ask questions that begin with: "How do you feel about...? What is your understanding of...? What do you believe the meaning of this is...?"

Let's say your child wants to go to a party where you believe there will be drinking and drugs. If you tell your child he can't go to the party because you think there will be drinking and drugs he may feel defensive or put down. You might say, "Thanks for asking, but for some reason I feel uneasy about you going. What do you think may be causing me to feel this way?" This gives your child the opportunity to discuss the family's personal morals and apply them without feeling personally judged.

A final way we can show our children unconditional love is by being positive role models for them. Children learn by observing how we act, and what we do is going to be the way our children learn to behave. We teach our children to serve by serving others, forgive by forgiving others, and to love by loving others. When we exemplify love and kindness, are of good cheer, engage in uplifting others, and bringing them joy and peace, our children will learn by our example and our behavior to do the same. What we want them to be, we must be.

Saying I'm Sorry

CHAPTER FIVE

Saying I'm Sorry

Heartfelt[1]

"I need to say something."
"I'm sorry."
"I am ready to listen and not judge."

A heartfelt sorry opens up the heart
For both parties."

Cambria Inouye

Saturday with a Teenage Daughter[2]

Written by Doris Jehnke, reprinted with permission

"Are you going to sleep all day?...Who said you
could use my hairspray?...Clean the dishes off the

table...Turn down the radio...Have you made your bed?...That skirt is much too short...Your closet is a mess...Stand up straight...Somebody has to go to the store...Quit chewing your gum like that...Your hair is too bushy...I don't care if everybody else does have one...Turn down the radio...Have you done your homework?...Don't slouch...You didn't make your bed...Quit banging on the piano...Why don't you iron it yourself?...Your fingernails are too long...Look it up in the dictionary...Sit up straight...Get off the phone now...Why did you ever buy that record? Take the dog out...You forgot to dust that table...You've been in the bathroom long enough...Turn off the radio and get to sleep now."

Another day gone, and not once did I say, "I love you."

Dear Lord, forgive me."

I believe a very important thing we can do for our children is to say I'm sorry when we make a mistake (which is pretty often). Children need to know their parents aren't perfect, and that they, too, are sorry for the mistakes they make. In talking to a lot of children, many tell me that they wish their parents would say, "I'm sorry." As a father I am constantly saying I'm sorry to my children. Most of the time it's because I'm angry at something else and I lose my temper with them. I can be mad at a client or have had a bad experience on the freeway and I will take it out on my children. I get so angry with myself for doing it, and I make sure I apologize to my children and let them know it was my problem that I took out on them. I have posters in my room to help me remember to keep my temper in check and leave my problems at the door.

On Father's Day I wrote each of my children a letter. Here is a letter I got back from my oldest son:

Dear Dad,

You are the best dad in the world. I'm sure no other dad would think of giving a letter to his kids on Father's Day. I love you a lot and I hope you know that you spend more time with me than most dads do and you always say sorry after you yell or get mad. I hope you know what a good job you are doing raising me and my brothers and sisters. You really are a good dad. Happy Father's Day.

Love, Shane

Saying "I'm sorry" to your kids doesn't mean you are weak. It shows that you care and you are trying to be a better parent. Your kids will see you as a bigger person and a better person for admitting you made a mistake.

Importance
o
f
H
u
g
s

CHAPTER SIX

The Importance of Hugs

Hugs[1]

Come close to me
Feel me, touch me
Hug me

It tells me
You approve of me
You're proud of me
And, best of all
That you love me

Cambria Inouye

More than one million children run away each year.
More than 30,000 commit suicide each year. There are

1,000,000 teen pregnancies each year. There are a great many alcohol-related deaths. More than 17,000 people die each year while driving intoxicated. We are seeing more mental hospitals, child abuse centers, and rape/assault hotlines. I have interviewed many policemen. I asked what they thought was the biggest cause of children and families spinning out of control. They all said the same thing: children have no supervision, and their parent beats their mate in front of them. We need to do whatever we can to make and keep our families strong.

These statistics are alarming. I believe that hugs are essential for life. Everyone needs human contact. Doctors have said that four hugs a day are necessary for life. My wife and I make sure we are getting and giving hugs to each other and our children on a daily basis. My brother and I created the "Hug Card" that was based on a booklet he wrote in 1986. Those who purchased the booklet wanted the little Hug Card that was on its cover. We took the card and marketed it. The card could be found in gift and novelty shops around the country and stores could not keep the Hug Cards in stock. This showed us what a need there was for such a positive product on the market. This product had a positive influence on a lot of people.

We received thousands of letters from teenagers thanking us for developing the Hug Card. One letter we received said, "As I grew older, my parents stopped hugging me, and with this card, it became easy to ask for a hug." We have sold over three million cards in the past thirteen years and hope they are still being used today. I hope you will use the card you get with this book, not only with your spouse, but also with your children. It is important for parents to show a lot of affection toward their children. I remember, as a high school student, kids would see us hug or kiss our parents as they dropped us off in the morning. We were all athletes and most of our athletic friends wished they had a relationship like that with their parents. Many fathers are afraid that if they hug and kiss their sons they will have sons with effeminate tendencies. The truth is quite different. It has been proven that fathers who hug and kiss their sons will have positive thinking, well-adjusted sons.

I have also heard fathers say they want their boys to be tough. "If their sons cry, they call them big babies or sissies. Boys have feelings too, and they need to show their emotions. It relieves a lot of stress and helps them to deal with their problems. Keeping emotions inside is not good for anyone. It can cause anger, resentment, even physical problems. It's great to cry. By not letting your children cry, you teach them to hold all their feelings in. This can cause them to be angry because they need to release their emotions somehow. I know a man who said, "I don't need to hug my sons because they'll turn out to be big sissies." Many people think its' OK for girls to cry, but not OK for boys to cry, and that's wrong. When our children are sad or upset, we encourage them to cry because it helps them to release their feelings and emotions. It took me a long time to get to that point because I used to tell my boys the exact same thing this other father did. I finally realized how important it was to show these feelings and emotions.

"Ask Your Children"

I sat down with each one of my children privately and asked them what made them happy. They all said different things. Some said watching television, some said eating junk food, but the one thing they had in common was the fact that they enjoy hugs and kisses, both those they give and receive, and those my wife and I give each other. Hugging comes easy for me because I like to do it. I enjoy hugging my wife and children. Thousands of psychologists have said how important human contact is. We don't need anyone to tell us how important hugs are. Look at the news. Runaways, drugs, suicide and prostitution all cover the headlines. It is never too late to start hugging. Make it a daily habit. You will see a change in your family and yourself. It seems like the only time people hug is when they haven't seen someone for a long time or there is some kind of tragedy. No family I know is perfect, but why not have a little bit of heaven in your home? With the world changing so much, it's nice to know that home can be a place of peace and love. It is interesting that something so easy to do can be so hard for so many people. No matter what time of day we turn the news on, 99% of the time it is negative. We have become a society with so much that is x-rated.

Thirteen years after selling the very first Hug Card, we

received a letter from a woman in Riverside. She purchased one of the first Hug Cards that were printed and wanted to buy more. She said she has kept it in her wallet all this time and the crystal on it is no longer good. She had no way of finding a new card and hoped we would be able to help her. People who have kept these cards in their wallets and have used them are still showing the need for positive influences.

Here is how the Hug Card works. The Hug Card is a temperature sensitive liquid crystal device that tells you how many hugs you need each day. If the Hug Card turns black, red, or green, it is indicating that your blood supply is being drawn inward. This is a natural physical process usually associated with daily tension. Obtain the minimum number of hugs indicated by the color chart to begin to feel refreshed and energized. Continue receiving hugs until the crystal turns blue. Repeat this exercise daily. If the Hug Card turns blue, the warm temperature in your fingertips indicates that you feel great. Share your positive energy with friends and loved ones by giving at least one hug away. Continue giving away hugs until the card turns blue for them, too. Repeat daily.

"What, oh what, can I give you????
Gold and silver, I have not,
Nor plantations or castles or fortune,
Finally I have thought of something special....
A big, big hug right from the heart!!!!

No moveable parts, no batteries needed
No periodic checkup, low energy consumption.

No insurance requirements, theft-proof.
Non-taxable, non-polluting
And of course, fully returnable!!!!

Hugging is healthy, it relieves tension
Combats depression, reduces stress,
Improves blood circulation, is invigorating,

Rejuvenating...it elevates self-esteem.
It generates good will.
It has no unpleasant side effects,
It is nothing less than a MIRACLE DRUG."

Sister Esther[3], the Nun

Hug (hîg) v. hugged, hugging, hugs.[4]
-tr.
1. To clasp or hold closely, especially in the arms, as in affection; embrace.
2. To hold steadfastly to; cherish.
3. To stay close to.

-intr.
1. To embrace or cling together closely.

-hug n.

1. A close, affectionate embrace.
2. A crushing embrace, as in wrestling. –huggable adj. – hugger n.

It is nice to see that the definition of hug includes affection. I believe it is very important not to just hug quickly, but to hug and hold to show the person that you really care about him or her.

"Daily Exercise"

These are the 5 steps on the **Power of Positive Hugging**:

1. Always hug your spouse in the morning and evening.

2. If you don't like hugs because you use the excuse that your parents never hugged you, start today and make it a daily exercise to hug as often as you can.

3. It has been said that we need four hugs a day for survival. Whether we give them or get them, you can never overdose on hugs.

4. It is never too late to start hugging your children. If you have never hugged your kids, start now. Make it a daily exercise.

5. While hugging your children, don't make it a quick
    hug with no affection. Show them that you care.
    Hold them tight every time. I remember a time when
    my wife was holding our youngest child and my 12-
    year-old son came up to her and said, "I miss being
    held like you hold the baby." My wife pulled him in
    her arms and held him for 15-20 minutes. Turn off
    the television, computers, etc. and pay attention to
    your children. Hug them. You will not believe the
    change it will have on their lives.

"Hugs for Happiness"

Studies have been done with people who have anorexia.
These people were thought to be near death and beyond hope.
One woman began doing hug therapy with them. She would
hold them, hug them, and whisper positive things to them.
These people began to heal and to view themselves more
positively. It is miraculous what some positive attention
can do. Follow these basic steps, and I guarantee that your
kids will be well adjusted, get better grades, have more self-
esteem, and be able to deal with day-to-day situations more
effectively. If you only take one thing away from this book,
I hope it is the knowledge that hugging is essential for life.
It is important to our well-being. I'm not perfect and I don't
always have the perfect answers to child rearing. I make
mistakes every day, but I do know that hugs are one of the
most important things we can do to and for each other.

The following article describes the "Hug Card" and the positive influence hugging can have on people. Some letters are also attached with testimonials on the power of hugging.

They're hoping the world will go hug wild

Hug Card signals when one is needed

Ed Norgord / Star-News

Hug card inventors Brent, left, and Barlow Hatch with wives Phelecia, Kathi

By LOUISE EGAN STEELE
Feature Writer

For two San Gabriel brothers it's thumbs up this Christmas shopping season. For each of the 50,000 customers who have bought The Hug Card so far, it's a thumb down on the little black square in the middle.

In fact, in the last six weeks the public has so fondly embraced the $2 hug-need detector that its young creators, Barlow and Brent Hatch, are sending 300,000 more into the national market. And it's their dearest hope that the whole world will go hug wild.

Just the size to slip in a wallet between a charge card and a driver's license, the plastic card registers one of four different colors after a 10-second hold of a thumb on its black square. If green, red or black, the owner of that thumb needs one to three squeezes. If it turns a happy blue, he/she should reach out and hug somebody.

The secret of the their creation, explained Barlow, is in the hand of the holder. If the person is depressed or negative, his or her blood is drawn inward, causing cold hands which flash the green, red or black signal that a reassuring hug is needed fast. On the other hand, the warm one, positive feelings turn the square into an embraceable blue.

"The world's fastest-selling gift item," as Barlow, 25, and Brent, 24, refer to their plastic brain child, has made them the happiest guys in the area. Colored or their thumbs bright blue. The 20 cards mounted on a display rack have been placed in florists, gift shops and bookstores not only locally but throughout the country. And some of the owners, reports Barlow, report sellouts before the first day is over. He added:

"Psychologists have proven that hugs are necessary and our cards help promote this positive experience for people."

And thinking positively is a way of life for the Hatches, two of the 13 children (all of whose first names begin with a "B") of nationally known motivational speaker Bill and wife Linda of Temple City.

"We were brought up to believe that we could do anything we made up our minds to do. On every desk in the house was one of Dad's inventions. One was a small can with a beautiful blue eye on top with the message, 'I can.'"

Shortly after graduation from Temple City High School Barlow started accompanying his father to various parts of the country on speaking engagements at corporations, educational institutions, church groups and national trade associations. At first he chauffeured his father and made arrangements for accommodations in various cities.

The more he listened to the inspirational messages of the forums and chatted with other speakers — the Rev. Norman Vincent Peale, for one — the more determined he was to follow in his father's footsteps onto the podium.

The young Hatch became known on the circuit, even acting as an emcee for many of the programs. He decided he'd like to give motivational lectures on his own. He was told that he couldn't be hired until he had a reputation in the field. Maybe a published book or two on the subject?

Remembering the tin can with the beautiful eye and its message underneath, he sat right down and wrote "I Can," and ▮▮▮▮▮ half million copies.

In the meantime, brother Brent had put his automobile manicuring specialty to work in his own business, "Perfection Detailing," where owners of wonder wheels in and around San Marino seek artistic denting and intricate finishing touches.

Both brothers, though, have put their other work aside for a time to concentrate on the business details of their huggable best-seller. They've named their motivational products company, "I Can and Associations."

Giving wifely assistance to the operation are Barlow's Kathi, the mother of their 3-month-old Chad, and Brent's Phelecia, who will soon add another grandchild to the Hatch family.

UNIVERSITY OF CALIFORNIA, IRVINE

BERKELEY · DAVIS · IRVINE · LOS ANGELES · RIVERSIDE · SAN DIEGO · SAN FRANCISCO SANTA BARBARA · SANTA

DEVELOPMENTAL BIOLOGY CENTER   IRVINE, CALIFORNIA   92717

July 30, 1987

Dear Mssrs. Hatch:

I ran into your credit card style hug card and really liked
it.   I have a friend who could benefit from one immensely.
I would like to get her one.   How do I get one of these?
Can you send me one?   Please send one or information on how
to obtain one.

Thank you,

June 5, 1989

Gentlemen:

We are the Mind Mint. We are also a Hypnotherapy Clinic and one
of our clients came into the clinic for treatment and he had one
of your "huggin" cards.

We were definitely impressed and so he said he had been told that
we could buy them from you.

Would you kindly send us back information on the quantities,
delivery and costs of this product?

Very truly yours

dmt;dmt

Dear sirs,
I just happened upon one of your HUG CARDS I was really mad and it made me feel better in a matter of one or two minutes . I would like to get 5 of them,one for each of my family . Please send me a catalog with prices,thank you.

April 30 1987

Please send me 12 - "A Hug Card".
This AM - a inmate was lodged & had
this card on him. Of course everyone
had to try it. We found the people that
had been here the longest - needed the
most hugs. I then read what was written
on the back of card - We decided to send
for some - I think this is a great idea.
Enclosed is check for $18.00.

Thank you very much

Jailer with Douglas Co Sheriff Dept

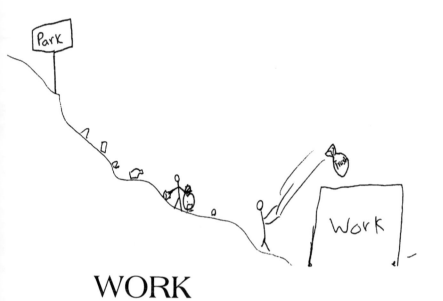

WORK

CHAPTER SEVEN

Work

Work can be so hard and not knowing
While you're going through it, that
You're getting stronger and wiser while
You do it.[1]

Cambria Inouye

Youngsters go beyond lemonade business...[2]
This story is reprinted from the Star News about my children

These kids aren't going to do the lemonade stand bit. Hey, it's 2000, and you just can't make enough doing that. Same for raking leaves, cutting lawns. Better to be day trading.

And for their Dad, Brent Hatch of South Pasadena, that's just fine. It's never too early to get a good grasp of a real money-making business. Hatch calls it "opportunities to earn."

Two of Hatch's six kids, Chari 11, and Shane 12, have

started a bounce castle business. And their father swears they're doing most of it themselves. Except for the driving, of course.

Bounce castle are those inflatable things you see at backyard parties and park gatherings. Kids go in there and jump off their lunch. Companies all over the place will charge you $100 a day or maybe even much more for the use of these things. They deliver them and pick them up at the end of the day.

After the initial investment of the castles, it's a pretty easy business. Mostly weekend work except for in the summer.

Because of this, and because of the fact that renting out bounce castles can give kids lessons in scheduling, product delivery, reliability and money management (and much more of that than a lemonade stand makes), Hatch decided to let them give it a go.

He invested in a castle and $1 million insurance policy and now they're putting up fliers at recreation centers, churches etc., advertising their new business.

Shane, a computer enthusiast and aspiring Web designer, used the Internet to help create the fliers they are using to promote their company, called Dr. Bounce. Chari will make the appointments and do the scheduling. Shane will also help with delivery, setup and takedown of the machines. They'll both learn a lot about money management.

Dr. Bounce came from their Dad's auto detailing business called Dr. Detail. Seemed like a natural.

"This is a good way to teach kids self-reliance," Hatch says, who keeps stressing that the kids are going to do most of this themselves. Hatch says his own business takes up enough of his time, thank you. And remember, he and wife Phelecia have seven kids total.

Dr. Bounce will charge $75 for the castle for up to eight hours. That sounds pretty reasonable. If they make a go of the business they'll buy more castles so they can make more appointments.

It could last the kids through high school and maybe even college.

Right now, Chari says she will bank her money when they start making it.

"This is just to make money to buy a laptop," Shane assures me.

But I also suspect some of Shane's profits will go in the bank if Dad has anything to say about it.

Up until now, both kids have been doing odd jobs for relatives and friends to make money. Shane cleans an aviary for $7 an hour.

Sounds like the Dr. Bounce business will be complex enough to have Chari and Shane get the experience of handling a decent sum of money. It will also be a great lesson in keeping the customer happy.

It is important for my children to do things for their neighbors and their community. We had a new neighbor move in across the street. He is an older man, and our street has huge trees that continually drop leaves. They can pile up a foot high. I got my kids together and said, "Do you see Henry across the street? Do you see those leaves over there? It's probably going to take thirty bags to clean it all up. I want the oldest three to go across the street and clean up his yard." I told them they could not accept any money and that it would be hard work, but they would feel better for helping someone. The neighbor was shocked and surprised and wanted to give them money, but they wouldn't accept it. That is something we can do with our children on a daily basis: teach them to serve others because when you're serving others, it helps you become a better person.

It is also very important to teach children to work hard. Work never killed anyone. We have chores for each of our children to do. It's not important that they are done perfectly, what's important is that the children are learning how to work. I know that if our children see their mother and father working hard, they will want to. As a family, we are trying to make work important starting at a young age.

Twelve Rules for Raising Delinquent Children[3]

Compiled from the Houston Police Department

1. Begin with infancy to give the child everything he wants. In this way he will grow up to believe that the world owes him a living.

2. When he picks up bad words, laugh at him. This will make him think he's cute.

3. Never give him any spiritual training. Wait until he is 21 and then let him "decide for himself."

4. Avoid the use of the word "wrong." It may develop a guilt complex. This will condition him to believe later, when he is arrested for stealing a car, that society is against him and he is being persecuted.

5. Pick up everything he leaves lying around—books, shoes, and clothes. Do everything for him so that he will be experienced in throwing all responsibility on others.

6. Let him read any printed matter he can get his hands on. Be careful that the silverware and drinking glasses are sterilized, but let his mind feast on garbage.

7. Quarrel frequently in the presence of your children. In this way they will not be too shocked when the home is broken up later.

8. Give a child all the spending money he wants. Never let him earn his own. Why should he have things as tough as you had them?

9. Satisfy his every craving for food, drink, and comfort. See that every sensual desire is gratified. Denial may lead to harmful frustration.

10. Take his part against neighbors, teachers, and police-
    men. They are all prejudiced against your child.

11. When he gets into real trouble, apologize for yourself
    by saying, "I never could do anything with him."

12. Prepare for a life of grief. You will be likely to have it.

"Work Hard"

I have a client who worked hard most of his life and
made good money. He has a 25,000-square-foot home and
many nice cars. One day, while doing a job for him, I began
to ask him how he acquired all of his wealth. He told me he
earned his money by owning his own business. I asked him
if he had any advice for a young entrepreneur like myself.
He said, "Whatever you do, spend time with your children
and make them work hard." He never made his children work
and gave them everything they wanted, he worked so they
didn't have to. When his children grew up, they couldn't
function in the real world and became mixed up in drugs.

I realize there is not a direct correlation between a child
being given everything and turning to drugs, but I have seen
and been told by many people that giving their children everything was the biggest mistake they ever made. Their children never learned to be responsible for anything or to take
pride in what they did. They did not take pride in themselves because they were never placed in a situation that

allowed them to feel like they had accomplished something. This led to low self-esteem and lack of pride, so, when faced with the situation of taking drugs or turning them away, they took the drugs. I have had people tell me I make my children work too hard. Living on a farm when I was young, I saw my Mom and Dad working hard all the time. I didn't always want to work, but I know it helped me be responsible. It's hard to be lazy when you see your parents working hard to put food on the table and give you clothes. I always tell my kids that when you work it makes you feel good. Working hard helps you feel like you've accomplished something. Hard work is not just on-the-job physical labor; homework and scouting and sports are hard work, too.

My oldest son and daughter don't always like to work, and I often tell them I don't like to work either. I do it because I have a responsibility to our family. Our family is a team, and we all have to work together to do a great job. I have had people approach me while doing yard work and say, "It's nice to see young kids doing hard work." Too many parents rob their children of the opportunity to learn hard work. It is so important for our children to see us work whenever possible. I'm lucky because I own my own business, and my children often have the opportunity of seeing me work. I feel it gives them a great appreciation of what I do for our family.

People often ask me how I am going to put all of my children through school. My parents raised 13 children and didn't have the means to help us through school. We are all doing well. We have either worked our way through school or started our own businesses. It is my responsibility to feed, clothe, provide shelter and love my children, but I think they should work their own way through school either through scholarships or outside jobs. I will help them with what I can, but I want them to learn to succeed on their own. I heard of a company that questions young applicants when they apply for jobs how they made it through college. The owner of the company wanted to know if they paid for their own education. Those who did were often hired over the ones whose parents put them through school. He believed they would work harder because they had achieved the goal of a college education by themselves. Having to gain things on our own teaches us to appreciate what we have and be respectful of it.

Some of the greatest experiences I have had working with my children were when we were adding onto our home. My brother and another person, my best friend, would come over and help me work, and many times my children would ask if they could help. They would beg to help and many times I wanted to tell them no because I had so much work to get done, but I took a few moments out of my time and let them help. I had them nail in nails, drill holes or help with clean up. Those are the times I cherish the most because they felt proud of their accomplishments, and they could see the payoff of all their hard work. It was something we were able to accomplish as a family. Parents need to make learning a positive experience for their kids.

When I am negative towards my children regarding a job they helped me with, it often puts them in a bad mood and they begin to criticize the rest of the family. My oldest daughter built a candy shop out of balsa wood. It took her about three days to complete it. I was helping her and wanted to whip through it as quickly as possible, but my wife reminded me that our daughter needed to learn how to do it herself. It seemed like it took forever, but when she was finished she was so proud of her accomplishment. It meant everything to her and I thought about what a great learning tool that situation was for both of us. It taught her hard work and persistence, while it taught me patience. It is also important that we don't spoil our children. By giving our children too much, we distort their values. By giving them everything, we take away their anticipation of working towards something.

My oldest son wanted a video game. I told him that when I was young my parents made me earn money for the things I wanted and, by doing that, those things meant more to me. I could have bought him the video game easily, but he would not have learned from it. My son earned the money to buy the video game by working at his grandmother's, caring for birds in her aviary, doing chores around the house, and doing artwork on the computer for a local company. He was very proud of his hard work. I am trying to teach my children the difference between wants and needs. On that farm in Diamond Valley, California, where I grew up, we were always given "hand-me-downs." It wasn't important to me to always have nice clothes. These days, it costs as much to buy a pair of shoes as my mom spent on dressing all thirteen of us.

It is important for us to help our children, but we must not go overboard. Many teenagers today feel they are entitled to the easy life because everything was always handed to them. A very important lesson to teach our children is that by helping those less fortunate than us, we receive many things in return.

Once, when my family was small (we only had two children then), we walked to the ice cream store. A homeless person was sitting on the corner asking for money. My young son without thinking twice, took his ice cream money out of his pocket and gave it to the man. I could not believe my small child had learned such a great thing. It is so important to help those in need because you never know when you may need help yourself.

I have four guidelines that I use to help teach my family:

1. Don't confuse what you want with what you need.

2. Avoid spoiling your children too much.

3. Live within your means and avoid unnecessary debt.

4. Give to others because when you help others you help yourself.

CHAPTER EIGHT

Family

In putting this book together, I decided to turn the word family into an acronym. I wanted those letters to stand for something and this is what I came up with:

Fathers

And

Mothers

In

Loving

Yourself

I thought this was great because I see so many parents out there who act like they can't stand their children. These parents really can't stand themselves. How can you give love when you don't have love for yourself? You have to have love in your heart for yourself as well as your family. I believe fathers and mothers cannot love their children unless they love themselves. If you, as a parent, don't have love in your heart, then how can you love your children and teach them to love? Joy and happiness are paramount to a happy family. Critical, upset, negative people will pass these feelings on to their children.

"Time"

We are in a crisis everyday with mothers neglecting their children and fathers abandoning their families. I always think I need to be someone great, or someone famous for my children to think I am an important person, but all my children want is for me to spend time with them, and love and respect them. They want a dad. The only people it's important for me to be great for are my children. Time is a very important issue for children. They don't want money, toys, or material possessions that many busy parents often try to give their children to make up for not being there. The most important gift we can give them is quality time. I have a friend who says, "I wish I could spend more time with my children. I'm so busy and we only have a small window of time each day." Our kids are growing up each day and they don't wait for us to find more time to spend with them. If we are too busy to spend time with our children, we need to step back and look at our priorities. The children need to see that Mom and Dad can have fun, too.

The more time we put into our families, the more happiness we will have in our lives.

You're never too old to change, so follow these 10 basic steps to a happier life, successful parenting, and bettering yourself:

1. Have genuine, unconditional love.

2. Have weekly, family get-togethers. Pick one day of the week where you teach your kids good morals.

3. Once a month, take each child aside to have a one-on-one conversation. Go over goals or discuss anything that is on your child's mind.

4. Hug always. Remember the power of positive hugging (Chapter 6).

5. Spend time with your family. The time you give your child is priceless.

6. Supervise your children. Always know what they are doing.

7. Respect your children. In order to get respect you need to give it.

8. Set goals.

9. Teach honesty.

10. Perform "random acts of kindness."

BEING POSITIVE

CHAPTER NINE

Being Positive

Good Night Gift[1]

"Good night my sweet boy.
I touch then hold his hand and squeeze,
"I like you
I love you
You're so beautiful deep inside
I like the way you overcome your
Challenges
You're so kind
You try so hard
You come up with the funniest jokes
You're a great big brother
I love being around you," I say.
"Mom, I'm a great person,"

he responds.
"Yes, you are!"
I return."

Cambria Inouye

The following is a story that has affected how I deal with our children.

Give Me a House[2]

Reprinted with permission from Bookcraft, 1971- 1999

"Give me a house with that lived-in look. Give me a house where no one is worried about the first scratch on the furniture because the second and third scratches are already there.

Give me a house where every book and magazine is not neatly put in a bookcase or magazine rack, but you find them scattered around in a sort of orderly profusion.

Give me a house where you may find the fingerprints of a child on a front window or door, or pick up a ball glove from a chair while ordering someone to put away his skates.

Give me a house with a few dirty dishes on the table, or an empty pop bottle standing upright on the floor beside the easy chair.

Give me a house where you can't find the evening paper until you first find out who had it last.

Give me a house that isn't too peaceful and quiet, a house where there are arguments over the use of the telephone, a house where western guns blaze away on the TV screen.

Give me a house where the children speak up to their parents, but don't talk back to them; where the parents listen to the children, but don't always give in to them.

Give me a house where everyone knows his rights and everyone respects his obligations.

Give me that kind of a house, and I'll show you a home—a happy home.²"

Being positive is very important in rearing children. I grew up in a family where we were always told we could do it. My wife is very good at saying positive things all the time, and I'm working more on recognizing that being positive is important to my children's happiness. To pray as a family at morning and night is very important. It helps us to have a positive outlook on life and to remember the happy things.

"Positive Attitudes"

Having a positive attitude requires constant work. It can be hard to be positive all the time, but it's so important because your kids are only going to act out what they see. If you are depressed and negative and always criticizing, they will do the same. If you have moldy food and put good food next to it, in a few days the good food will be moldy. I try to be as positive as I can with our kids. Happiness is a state of mind. Lincoln once said: "We are as happy as we make up our minds to be." When I go home, I try to leave my problems out on the fence and concentrate on feeling the needs of my family. When my children have problems, I really listen to what they say. If we concentrate on each child's feelings, helping them feel special, they will have much more self-esteem. I know that when they leave for school they will have a much better day because I took the time to lift them up.

People in the world are not always going to be positive, so we need to be positive at home. Our children will then see how positive attitudes can make us happy. One of our daughters used to come home from school sad and upset. She had a teacher who always yelled at the kids. My wife is not a yeller so my daughter wasn't used to an adult yelling at her. My wife went to school a little early and heard the teacher putting the students down in a way that was not appropriate. My wife took the teacher aside and told her how much damage she was doing to our daughter, as well as the other children. After a long talk with my wife, the teacher said her mom always yelled at her and that she didn't even realize what she was doing. She gave my wife a hug and thanked her for bringing this to her attention.

It is hard not to be negative toward your kids, but you should always remember to tell them how well they are doing. Remember, we only get one chance at being good parents so let's make the most of it and do the best we can. When I was a coach for my son's baseball team, I concentrated on what my son, the player, couldn't do rather than building a relationship and memories with him. I was constantly on him in a negative manner. I knew he didn't enjoy going to baseball because of this, and realized he was unhappy. So, the next few games, I tried to say only encouraging things. His attitude changed and he loved baseball again. I asked why he was doing so much better at sports. He said it was because I was always bringing him up in a positive way and not getting upset.

Raising a family is like having a bank account. If you put in a little bit of money, in twenty years you will have a fair amount, but if you put in a lot of money, you will have much more. The same goes for children. If you put in a great deal of time with them when they are young, they will be good to you when they're older. I have talked with many parents who can't understand why their kids don't come over or talk much anymore. I then come to find out that most of these parents didn't spend much time with their children. They were busier making money than making relationships. "Much happiness was overlooked because it doesn't cost anything."

A Child's Hope[3]

A child not knowing where to go,
not knowing who's friend or foe.
All she wants to do is hide.
She is hurting so deep inside.

Longing for someone to hold.
Hugging herself, feeling so cold.
"I'm alone, I'm alone," she cries.
Reaching in desperation, tries.

"What should I do?"
"Reach and trust in who?"
Don't you want it to be you?
You're the one who loves her so.
Hold her, hug her, don't let her go.
No matter how hard she can be,
let her know you would never flee.

Take her by the hand and explain,
through her trials there's only strength to gain.
Through the years
there will be lots of tears.
Teaching by example
when life's sin she wants to sample.

Telling her right from wrong.
Showing her how to be strong.
Building with love day by day.
One day she will look at you and say,
"You were there through the years,
hugging me through the tears,
helping me grow and learn.
Now that it is my turn,

All your love you did sow.

I'll never be alone.

I know I'm always welcome home.

I never have to hide,

feeling so much love inside.

I know a hug there always will be.

You've been the best parents to me."

Cambria Inouye

I always remember having a positive motivational attitude in my life. When we were young, my Dad took a can and glued eyes all over it. He called it the eye can. Anytime we said we couldn't do it, he would point to the can and ask "What kind of can is that?" We would answer, "It's a can." "Yes, but what kind of can?" "It's an eye can." He would make us say it over and over again until it sunk in. It's much more beneficial to have someone saying you can do it than to have someone telling you that you can't. It is much better for a child's self-esteem.

It is easy for us to forget how important it is to have an "I can" attitude. Sometimes it's okay to feel a little down so that when we are happy, we will appreciate the happiness. It is important, though, to work at having a positive attitude. I have been around people who always look at the negative in life. If it's a cloudy day, they focus on the negative aspects and complain about the weather. I have also been around people who look at that same day with joy and think what a fantastic day it is. It is so much better to look at things with a positive attitude.

What a wonderful world this would be if we all, as parents, told our children before they left for school how proud we are of them and encourage them to do a great job. When they came home that night, if we asked them how their day was and congratulated them on all of their accomplishments we would all be happier. Don't forget to keep the lines of communication open and uplift your children every chance you get.

"Perseverance"

A key to being positive and having a positive outlook on life is perseverance. Throughout my life I have never given up when trying to accomplish something, even if I thought I might fail. I am always up for the challenge, and with our children, I am trying to teach them that it's not the sport you play or the goal you're trying to achieve that's important. Trying your best and never giving up is what is most important.

Goals are very important to have. They help us to persevere. A goal not written down is only a wish. I believe goals are a way to push us to achieve something that is important to us. Without goals we have no focus. At a young age, I remember my dad had a picture of a very well built man taped to his mirror. After a lot of hard work he looked like that man. He also wanted a nice car, and finally the goal came true. As a young father, I know that goals are extremely important at a young age. At around four or five years of age, I began asking my kids what kind of goals they have, what they want to be when they grow up, and things of that nature. It is very important with young children to set any kind of goal, whether it be taking out the trash, cleaning their room, or helping with dinner. We would write all of their goals down. We would always go over their goals, whatever they might be. We try to do this once a month. I would ask them to set goals that are not too high, so they wouldn't get disappointed and feel they failed if they couldn't reach that goal. Another important thing about this was the fact that we were having father/son or father/daughter interviews. This was a time set aside where they knew they would have my undivided attention, and they could talk to me about anything. It is so important in helping them grow and being able to keep their goals. It is also very important that you don't get angry at whatever they tell you because they need to know they can trust their parents. It is better for them to tell you than to tell a friend.

When I go over my children's goals with them, I make it a point to encourage them and tell them how important it is to do their best. My wife and I try to constantly reinforce the idea that you can do anything you want as long as you put your mind to it. My oldest son loves to cook. He loves it so much he is taking a cooking class at school. This can be handled in two ways. I can either make him feel proud of his interests and encourage him to be the best at cooking he can be, or I can look down on cooking and make negative comments about his interests. By doing that, not only will it help create a low self-esteem, but it will make him feel the things he is interested in are not important. It doesn't matter what our children do, it is up to us to make them feel important no matter what and to promote a positive mental image and attitude.

"Goals"

My young son, McKay, is in Kindergarten and he was showing us the goals he had set and his accomplishments. At first I said, "That's great," without even realizing what he had been saying. My wife told me to sit down with him and really pay attention to what he was telling me. He was so excited to show me all of the things he had accomplished and learned. If we, as parents, praise our children for the small things as well as the big ones, it will help to build strong self-esteem and make them want to naturally shoot for high goals. When I sit down with the kids to go over their goals, I write the goals on a 3x5 index card. These are kept in a plastic box, and we read them as often as possible. Some of the things we include on these index cards are promises the children make, not to my wife and me alone, but to themselves as well. One promise is, "I promise never to use drugs," with the child's signature at the end. Another promise for the boys is, "I promise to treat women with respect."

I hope we can continue this tradition even when my kids are teenagers, because goals are such an important part of life.

Conclusion

CHAPTER TEN

Conclusion

Many people in this world define success as having money, fame or nice things. That is far from the truth. There is nothing wrong with having money or nice things, but we need to put those things in perspective. There is a man my wife and I have known since we were married in 1985. He had a big home, big bank account, and everything material a person could want. He was missing one element that can make a person truly happy—a family. He and his wife put off having children so they could have nice things. We would have him over for dinner when we were still a small family, and he would tell us not to have more children. He said they were too expensive. When we had our third child he asked us how we could afford having such a big family on one person's income. With our fourth child he told us our house was too small to fit all of us. With our fifth all he did was laugh.

We hadn't heard from him for a while, but one day we were driving away from our home and saw him walking down our street. We stopped to talk to him and he told us that he had all the money he needed, but we had everything money couldn't buy. We were happy, healthy and we had children to take care of us. He said he wished he had had a family. One day, many years later, I stopped by his home, but he wasn't there. He had been sent away to a convalescent home where he died alone.

I know people who's children are involved with drugs or crime and who have said many times that they would sell everything they had to have their children back. It's funny how we work to have the finer things in life, but all we really need is usually right in front of us.

The Family of Success[1]

Reprinted with permission

"The father of Success is named Work.

The mother of Success is named Ambition.

The oldest son is called Common Sense, and some of the boys are called Stability, Perseverance, Honesty, Thoroughness, Foresight, Enthusiasm and Cooperation.

The oldest daughter is Character, Some of the sisters are Cheerfulness, Loyalty, Care, Courtesy, Economy, Sincerity and Harmony.

The baby is Opportunity.

Get acquainted with the father of Success, and you will be able to get along with the rest of the family. "

I am constantly working on being a better father. As we have said, "Anything worth doing requires a lot of work." This statement especially pertains to raising a family. I believe that there needs to be a balance between family and work. The happier your family is the more successful and happy you will be. I heard a quote once that said, "There are those who make money and those who make excuses. By the same token, there are those who make great families and those who make excuses." I have talked to a lot of people who have blamed their family failures on everyone but themselves. Ninety percent of what our kids learn and do is taught at home. I believe that if we teach our kids good, wholesome principles no matter where they go, they will always come back.

The Home is the Answer[2]
by Ray Taylor, Reprinted with permission, Bookcraft 1971-1999

A stabilized home, in which religious instruction plays a major part, is the only real answer to juvenile delinquency. This is the consensus of scholars who have made a serious study of the causes and prevention of delinquency. These scholars maintain that parents and children alike must be taught how to live together as a family—their home must be "God-centered," and must be associated with a church that provides an uplifting, character-building program for youth.

The scholars list two kinds of homes: one that produces delinquency, and the other that seldom has youth problems. The poor home in which delinquency thrives is described as one in which there is no genuine love between father and mother, nor between parents and children; no regular family routine in the home; no preparation, no planning; no fixed time for meals, no set time to come in at night, nor to do homework, nor to go to bed; no discipline nor rules of conduct; no group activity; and little or no religious and moral training.

Such a home usually has in it parents who drink and who give their own children liquor at home; parents who quarrel, even in the presence of their children; who party and carouse; who are often untruthful, dishonest, careless about paying bills, and who give their children no training in financial matters; who provide no companionship for children; and who have no respect for religious matters.

J. Edgar Hoover, former head of the FBI, explained that juvenile delinquency seldom results when young people are brought up in homes in which:

1. Parents try to understand their children and find time to cultivate their friendship and love.

2. Parents of integrity face facts and live by the truth.

3. Parents live within their means and give their children examples in thrift, security, and stability.

4. Parents are industrious and teach their children that most of life's good things come only from hard work.

5. Parents have worthwhile goals in life and seek to have their children join them in their attainment.

6. Parents have common sense, a capacity for friendship, and a sense of humor.

7. Parents live in harmony with each other and do not quarrel in front of children.

8. Parents have ideals and a compelling urge to serve rather than to be served.

9. Parents are unswervingly loyal to their own children, but can express righteous indignation and chastise them when necessary.

10. Parents' decisions are controlled not by what their children *desire*, but by what they *need*.

We must remember, as parents, that we cannot control our children, we can only teach them what's right, and let them know continually how much we love them. If we are good examples and a constant presence in their lives, we will be much more aware of danger signs that begin to surface when our children aren't doing what they know they should be doing. Also, if we are a constant presence in their lives, our children will be more apt to come to us with their concerns and fears.

There are as many definitions for success as there are people in this world. One person will say that success, to them, is money. Another will say fame. My wife and I believe success is having a healthy, happy family. Not everyone will achieve millionaire status, but the one thing we can all do, no matter what race, color or creed we are, is to have a successful family. It all starts with you. No one can take that from you. Loving our families and having good relationships with them should be our most important definition of success.

Hopefully, the things we have discussed in this book will help you on your journey to raising a good family. We truly live in an X-Rated world and are bombarded with its evils everyday. Be aware. Your children need you. We can honestly tell you these things work, because they are working for us. Remember that failure in the home cannot be compensated for by any other success.

Being G-Rated in an X-Rated world is a good thing. We see constant reminders every day that our children are living G-Rated lives and we wouldn't have it any other way.

Notes

Chapter 1
1. "The Meanest Mother," reprinted from KFI, NBC TV as compiled for Sharon and Stan Miller

Chapter 2
1. Poem written by Cambria Inouye

Chapter 3
1. Poem written by Cambria Inouye
2. Taken from the Pasadena Star News
3. Taken from the Internet

Chapter 4
1. Poem written by Cambria Inouye

Chapter 5
1. Poem written by Cambria Inouye
2. "Saturday with a Teenage Daughter," written by Doris Jehnke, as compiled by Stan and Sharon Miller

Chapter 6
1 Poem written by Cambria Inouye
2 Statistics taken from the Internet
3 Written by Sister Esther as compiled by Sharon and Stan Miller
4 Taken from Webster's Dictionary

Chapter 7

1 Poem written by Cambria Inouye
2 Written by Jason Schaff as taken from the Pasadena Star News
3 "12 Rules for Raising a Delinquent Child," Houston Police Department, as compiled by Sharon and Stan Miller

Chapter 9

1 Poem written by Cambria Inouye
2 "Give Me a House," as compiled by Sharon and Stan Miller
3 Poem written by Cambria Inouye

Chapter 10

1 "The Family of Success," as compiled by Sharon and Stan Miller
2 "The Home is the Answer," written by Ray Taylor as compiled by Sharon and Stan Miller

This is not the end . . .

It's the beginning

Life is GOOD!
Dana Suorsa

Read YOUR story in the Hatchs' next books!

The Hatchs' are putting together their next books, *Raising G-Rated Teens in an X-Rated World,* and *The Power of Positive Hugging.* They would like to hear from you.

✓ What kinds of problems have you encountered in raising your teens?

✓ Have you overcome these problems?

✓ What things have you learned in dealing with these problems?

✓ How do you communicate with your teens?

✓ How do you practice what you've learned?

✓ How has your relationship with your teens improved?

There is no limit on how much you write.

Please send your response to:
Dawson Publishing
P. O. Box 820
South Pasadena, CA 91031
(626) 441-0368
www.thehugdr.com

There are no guarantees your story will be used and all material sent will become property of Dawson Publishing.

FAMILY REPORT CARD

(A CHILD'S REPORT CARD ON THEIR PARENT'S BEHAVIOR)

CHILD'S NAME _____   PARENT'S NAME _____   RELATIONSHIP _____   DATE _____

ITEM	SUBJECT	MONTH 1	MONTH 2	MONTH 3	MONTH 4	MONTH 5	MONTH 6	Comments
1.	Do I spend enough time with you?							
2.	Do I listen enough?							
3.	Am I positive to you?							
4.	Are you proud of me as a parent?							
5.	Do I keep my promises?							
6.	Do I explain why I failed to keep my promises?							
7.	Do I yell too much?							
8.	Do I say I'm sorry enough?							
9.	Do you feel loved unconditionally?							
10.								
11.								
12.								
13.								
14.								

SEE THE REVERSE SIDE FOR INSTRUCTIONS ON HOW TO GRADE YOUR REPORT CARD.   Copyright © 2000 by Brent Hatch

Raising a
G RATED FAMILY
in an
X RATED WORLD

INSTRUCTIONS ON GRADING YOUR REPORT CARD.

This is a report card for our children to grade us as parents. Have your child fill out the report card, by giving you an A, B, C, D, or F. This needs to be done in a very non-threatening and loving environment. You want them to be able to be honest. After your child/children finish grading your report card, talk to them about why they chose the grades they did. Ask them how they think you can improve. Don't get angry if the grades are not what you thought they should be. Respond with kindness and love. The important thing is that you and your child/children are communicating in a positive way. No matter how you feel, let them grade you once every month or so, whatever is comfortable with your family.

Additional blank lines are included for you to personalize your report card to fit your family's needs.

A = Excellent
B = Above Average
C = Average
D = Below Average
F = Fail — if "F," begin work to improve in that area and have your children grade you monthly to track your progress. If no improvement is seen, seek professional help.

As a parent wouldn't it be a positive step to really know how your child feels about you; your strengths and weaknesses (everyone has them!); and how you can improve as a parent or parents. If you can take the time now to listen to your children's needs, then the regret won't come later. If more parents would give their children the opportunity to express their feelings about you, and truly be willing to change their actions, maybe there would not be the violence in our schools or in the world.

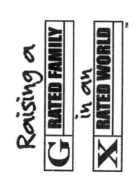

Raising a
G RATED FAMILY in an
X RATED WORLD ™

IF YOU HAVE QUESTIONS OR ARE INTERESTED IN ORDERING MORE REPORT CARDS, PLEASE CONTACT: DAWSON PUBLISHING, P. O. BOX 820, SOUTH PASADENA, CA 91031.

FAMILY REPORT CARD

(A CHILD'S REPORT CARD ON THEIR PARENT'S BEHAVIOR)

CHILD'S NAME PARENT'S NAME RELATIONSHIP DATE

ITEM	SUBJECT	MONTH 1	MONTH 2	MONTH 3	MONTH 4	MONTH 5	MONTH 6	Comments
1.	Do I spend enough time with you?							
2.	Do I listen enough?							
3.	Am I positive to you?							
4.	Are you proud of me as a parent?							
5.	Do I keep my promises?							
6.	Do I explain why I failed to keep my promises?							
7.	Do I yell too much?							
8.	Do I say I'm sorry enough?							
9.	Do you feel loved unconditionally?							
10.								
11.								
12.								
13.								
14.								

SEE THE REVERSE SIDE FOR INSTRUCTIONS ON HOW TO GRADE YOUR REPORT CARD. Copyright © 2000 by Brent Hatch

Raising a
G RATED FAMILY
X RATED WORLD

INSTRUCTIONS ON GRADING YOUR REPORT CARD.

A = Excellent
B = Above Average
C = Average
D = Below Average
F = Fail — if "F," begin work to improve in that area and have your children grade you monthly to track your progress. If no improvement is seen, seek professional help.

This is a report card for our children to grade us as parents. Have your child fill out the report card, by giving you an A, B, C, D, or F. This needs to be done in a very non-threatening and loving environment. You want them to be able to be honest. After your child/children finish grading your report card, talk to them about why they chose the grades they did. Ask them how they think you can improve. Don't get angry if the grades are not what you thought they should be. Respond with kindness and love. The important thing is that you and your child/children are communicating in a positive way. No matter how you feel, let them grade you once every month or so, whatever is comfortable with your family.

Additional blank lines are included for you to personalize your report card to fit your family's needs.

As a parent wouldn't it be a positive step to really know how your child feels about you; your strengths and weaknesses (everyone has them!); and how you can improve as a parent or parents. If you can take the time now to listen to your children's needs, then the regret won't come later. If more parents would give their children the opportunity to express their feelings about you, and truly be willing to change their actions, maybe there would not be the violence in our schools or in the world.

Raising a
[G RATED FAMILY]
in an
[X RATED WORLD]™

IF YOU HAVE QUESTIONS OR ARE INTERESTED IN ORDERING MORE REPORT CARDS, PLEASE CONTACT:
DAWSON PUBLISHING, P. O. BOX 820, SOUTH PASADENA, CA 91031.

Order Form

Book "Raising A G-Rated Family in an X-Rated World"
Price per copy: $9.95:
Quantity ordered_____@ $9.95 ea   = $_____
S/H $3.00 for the first book; $1.00 each additional book.
(Allow 3-4 weeks for delivery)   = $_____
              Subtotal   = $_____

"The Power of Positive Hugging" card
Price per card: $1.99
Quantity ordered_____ @ $1.99 ea   = $_____
S/H 50¢—up to 5 cards (50¢ per each
additional up to 5 cards) (allow 5-7 days)   = $_____
              Subtotal   = $_____

"The Family Report Card"
Price per package of 10: $2.00
Quantity ordered_____ @ $2.00 ea   = $_____
S/H $1.00 per package: (allow 7-10 days)
              Subtotal   = $_____
Sales Tax: CA residents add 8.25%   = $_____
          ORDER TOTAL   = $_____

Mail to:

Name_____

Address_____

City_____State_____ ZIP_____

Telephone (____)_____ _____

Order / Payment:
OnLine: **go to www.thehugdr.com**
By Check: make payable to: Dawson Publishing,
              P. O. Box 820, South Pasadena, CA 91031
Credit Card: check one • Visa • MasterCard • Discover

Card number:_____

Name on card:_____ **Exp. Date**_____

(for volume orders call (626) 441-0368)